The Usborne First
HISTORY BOOK

Jane Chisholm and Robyn Gee
Illustrated by Rob McCaig

Contents

Part 1
Prehistoric Times
Page 2

Part 2
Roman Times
Page 25

Part 3
Castle Times
Page 49

D1403202

Designed by Kim Blundell and Rob McCaig
History adviser: Dr Anne Millard

LIVING IN PREHISTORIC TIMES

Contents

Part 1:
2 How people lived 17,000 years ago
4 Moving for the winter
6 Winter
10 The snow melts
12 Summer

Part 2:
14 How people lived 7,000 years ago
16 Daytime
18 Evening
20 Shopping
21 Going hunting
22 Harvest time
24 Harvest festival

First published in 1982 by Usborne Publishing Ltd,
83-85 Saffron Hill, London EC1N 8RT, England.
Copyright © 1991, 1982 Usborne Publishing Ltd.
The name Usborne and the device ⛛ are Trade Marks of Usborne Publishing Ltd.

Printed in Belgium.

Part 1: How people lived 17,000 years ago

The first part of this book is about a 10 year old girl called Willow and her brother Hawk, aged seven.

Their story is set in southern France, about 17,000 years ago. The weather was much colder then. Huge areas of the world were covered with ice. Many countries were a slightly different shape too.

Hawk and Willow have a mother and father and 14 year old brother, Bison. They live with a lot of other relatives in a large group called a clan. Their clan is called the Reindeer Clan. It has about 100 people in it. They live as a large family and share a lot of their things.

There were far fewer people during Willow's time. You could go for months, or years, without seeing a stranger. People do not know how to grow food or tame animals for farming. So they hunt and fish and collect wild plants to eat instead. Willow does not live in the same place all year round. The animals move from season to season. So the clan follows them, in order to get food.

They always camp close to a stream, so they can get water.

Willow's grandfather is the clan chief. He lives in this hut.

Willow's mother, Berry, is roasting meat on a spit.

The clan has two main camps – one for summer and one for winter. In the summer, they live in huts that look rather like wigwams. The camp is not far from the sea. They do not stay here in winter, as it gets very cold and windy.

The snow has only just started to fall. It is often deeper than the height of a person.

A lot of people come here in winter, as it is a good area for hunting. A clan called the Bear Clan lives in these caves.

Salmon River

Willow's father is called Wolf. He is the chief hunter. He has just trapped a fox.

Here are some of the animals that live in the area. Nowadays many of them live further north, where it is colder. Some, like the mammoth, have died out completely.

◁ Reindeer

Mammoth ▽

△ Bear

Chamois ▽

△ Wild horse

Wolf ▽

△ Bison

In winter, the clan lives in a group of caves in a cliff on the edge of a river. They call it "Salmon River", because they catch a lot of salmon there in spring. It is much too cold to live in the open.

3

Moving for the winter

Wolf is carrying a piece of burning wood. They always try to keep something alight. Fires are difficult to light, as there are no matches.

At the beginning of autumn, herds of animals start to leave the valley where the Reindeer Clan is camped. They are heading inland. The Reindeer Clan follows them. They pack up their furs, tools and some food for the journey. The winter caves are many days' walk away.

When they arrive, they find a bear living in one of the caves. They manage to frighten it away with flaming branches. Animals are afraid of fire.

Collecting firewood

Building a wall

Leather tents

Willow's family are busy arranging their cave. They live close to the entrance because of the light. Hawk is building a wall of rocks to keep the wind out. Bison is putting up tents for sleeping in. The beds are made of fur and bracken. Uncle Bear digs a pit to store the food in. It will stay fresher underground.

Wolf is starting a new fire. He rubs two sticks together on top of a pile of leaves. The rubbing makes heat, which sets fire to the leaves.

4

The hunters make sure the wind is blowing towards them. This stops the animals from smelling them.

Wood

Leather binding

Sharp stone

This is a spear-thrower. It helps throw the spears much further.

They disguise themselves with reindeer skins and antlers, so as not to frighten the animals.

There is plenty to do at this time of year. The clan has to hunt and collect a lot of food to store for winter. When the snow falls, it will be more difficult to get around. Hawk and the other boys go hunting with the men. They are learning how to creep up on reindeer. Children do not have much time to play. They are given jobs to do instead.

Fur boots tied on with leather laces.

Willow is picking nuts and berries. The women in the clan are in charge of collecting wild plants to eat.

She digs up roots to eat with a special digging stick.

5

Winter

Winter lasts for many months (or "moons", as people call them). Most of the clan stay inside the cave, making tools and clothes. It is too cold to go out much.

Hawk's father is teaching him to make tools from a stone called flint. He is chipping away thin, sharp pieces. They can be used for things like knives or spearheads.

Leather thread

Willow is making necklaces from shells. These are useful for swapping for other things. There is no money. So clans swap furs, tools or shells for the things they need.

Someone has carved a picture of a mammoth and a reindeer on the cave wall.

Hawk's cousin, Eagle, is carving pictures of animals on his spear-thrower.

Hawk has made himself a whistle from a hollowed-out bone. It only plays a few different notes.

In the evening, everyone gathers round the fire while the meal is cooking. Grandfather entertains them with stories of hunting and adventure. The stories are based on things that really happened. But storytellers have added to them over the years, to make them more exciting. After supper, Hawk and Willow crawl into their tent to sleep.

The fire is kept burning all night. It helps keep them warm and scares away wild animals.

Aunt Heather is stirring the stew. It is made of wild boar and root vegetables. The pot is made from a carved-out tree trunk. Hot pebbles are dropped into the stew to heat it.

Willow's mother is sewing two pieces of fur together: First she makes holes in the fur with a piece of sharp, pointed stone. This makes it easier to sew. All their clothes are made of fur and leather.

Bone needle

Leather thread

Shells

The sewing is done with a bone needle and leather thread. Willow helps by sewing shells and animal teeth on to the clothes as decoration.

Cave painting

Uncle Larch is painting with an animal hair brush. Sometimes he uses his fingers too.

Stone palette for mixing the colours on.

Lamp

The paints are made from charcoal, earth, rocks and plants. The only colours are black and shades of red, brown and yellow.

A hollowed-out horn is used to store the paint.

The coloured earths are ground and mixed with fat and water.

The cave is very deep and full of passages. The deep parts are hardly ever used, as it is dark and easy to get lost. Every winter, some of the men go down one of the passages to paint pictures on the walls. They take stone lamps, which burn animal fat, to help them see. The pictures are mostly of animals and hunting scenes. The clan believe their lives are ruled by spirits. They hope the paintings will please the spirits and bring them luck.

Hunting in the snow

A leather noose is attached to a branch of a tree. The branch is bent over. The noose is looped round a bone, which is stuck into the ground. The bone is held in place by a rock.

Some food is left as a bait. When the animal walks into the noose, it pulls the loop off the bone. Then the branch springs back and the noose tightens round the animal.

They wear the fur on the inside. This keeps in the warmth better.

The men go out hunting in winter too, although the deep snow makes it more difficult. They have to put on extra clothes because of the cold. The stores of food in the cave can be used if they do not catch anything. Wolves and foxes are hunted for their fur. It is at its bushiest in winter and will be useful for making warm clothes. Here Hawk's father is showing him how to set a trap.

A ceremony

The boys dance round in a circle, miming animals.

This clay reindeer is the clan symbol.

The witchdoctor wears reindeer antlers and his face is painted.

Just before spring, a special ceremony is held in one of the deep parts of the cave. Some of the boys in the clan are now old enough to be counted as men in the next hunting season. The ceremony is held to celebrate this. Willow's brother, Bison, is one of the boys. A witchdoctor speaks to the spirits and asks them to accept the boys as men.

The snow melts

The new hunting season begins once the snow starts to melt. Hawk has broken his spear, so he is making a new one.

First he chooses the straightest branch he can find. He cuts off the uneven edges with a flint knife. Then he heats it, to harden it.

Bear's tooth necklace

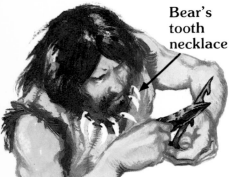

Wolf is making a harpoon to catch fish with. The harpoon head is made of bone. He carves hooks on to it with a sharp flint tool.

Tusks are used for carving things, such as spear-throwers or jewellery.

The trap was disguised with branches.

The hunters kill the mammoth with stones and spears. A mammoth is a good catch. It will feed the whole clan for weeks.

Mammoths eat trees, mosses and other plants.

In spring, herds of animals start to leave for their summer pastures. The hunters dig pit traps along the paths that the animals usually take. Here a mammoth has been caught. The clan do not see so many nowadays. The climate has slowly been getting warmer, over hundreds of years. Mammoths have been moving to colder places.

The women sit on the banks, cleaning and drying the fish.

Weir

These hooks stop the fish from wriggling free.

These children are collecting pebbles to use in cooking.

The baskets are made of woven river reeds.

Every spring, shoals of salmon swim up river to lay their eggs. They leap up mountain streams and waterfalls. Fish are much easier to catch in shallow water. Hawk and his father stand in the stream with their harpoons ready to spear the fish. Some of the other men have built a sort of weir from a circle of rocks. This traps the fish as they swim through.

Further downstream, the river widens and the water is very deep. It is hard to catch fish with harpoons here. Some of the Bear Clan are laying basket traps for the fish.

11

Summary

As summer comes, it is time to leave the caves and travel to the summer hunting grounds. The clan is heading for a valley on the west coast. They usually go to the same place every year. They wave good-bye to the Bear Clan, who are going to the Alps.

The Reindeer Clan set up camp here for the summer months. There are no caves in the area, so they build huts to live in. The huts are made from branches, covered with leaves, grass and animal skins. The ones they lived in last year have been destroyed by snow and ice.

Willow and her mother are making leather from animal skins. They stretch them and scrape them clean with a piece of stone. Then they leave them to dry.

Aunt Heather is preserving a piece of meat (to help it keep longer). It will be left over a smoky fire for several days.

Each summer, the men go on a "mountain drive". This means chasing a herd of animals over a cliff. The animals are killed immediately. It is a good way of building up a large supply of meat.

Bison and his friend are hunting partridges and grouse. They try to attract the birds by imitating their call.

Wild horses

Bathing in the sea and in rivers is the only way they have of washing. In winter, many of the rivers are frozen over and it is much too cold.

Willow collects the shells in a leather bag.

Hawk and Willow enjoy summer because it means plenty of trips to the beach. They go looking for shells to swap or use for making jewellery. In the rockpools, they sometimes find a lobster or crab or some small shellfish. They take these home to roast over the fire.

13

Part 2: How people lived 7,000 years ago

About 10,000 years have passed, since the time of Hawk and Willow.
Some people have learned how to grow food and tame animals. This means they can settle in one place, instead of moving around all the time.

This part of the book is about 10 year old Tupi and his eight year old sister, Shara. They live in a village in a part of the world we call Turkey.

In many places, people still live like the Reindeer Clan, hunting for all their food. But this way of life is more difficult now.

In Europe and other places, the ice has melted and the weather is getting warmer. Many of the animals people used to hunt have moved to colder climates. A lot of land is covered forest now and this makes the animals harder to spot.

This is Tupi and Shara's village. It has about 200 people in it and is ruled by a village chief. There is a thick wall around it, to keep out intruders. Each house has about three or four rooms. Some have a second floor, which you reach by step-ladder.

The pottery. People have learnt new skills since Willow's time. They now know how to make pottery and spin and weave.

Straw roof

Mud walls

Tupi's father is ploughing his field. Soon he will plant wheat and barley. Each family has a separate piece of land.

The animals are taken to the hills during the day, but are kept inside at night.

Oven

Village shrine. This is where people go to worship the goddess who looks after the village.

Tupi and Shara live in this house, with their mother, father, six year old brother, Sharbit, and baby sister, Kebbi.

Tupi's mother and Aunt Esha are laying out dates and figs to dry.

This family is building a new house. They have just moved here from another village. Their land had lost its goodness and stopped producing crops.

Dogs are kept as pets and used for rounding up animals. They were originally bred from wolves that people had tamed.

These are the animals that are kept in Tupi's village. They are very like the farm animals we have, except they are smaller and shaggier and their horns are longer. They were originally wild animals. But people began catching very young ones and taming them. Then they bred from the tamest and healthiest ones.

Goat

Pig

Cow

Goose

Duck

Sheep

Wheat and barley grow wild in the Middle East, where Tupi lives. People there discovered that they could grow more by collecting the seeds and planting them in good soil.

15

Daytime

Sling

Like many boys, Tupi's job is looking after the animals. Each morning he collects the sheep and goats from their pen and takes them into the hills. His dog, Marn, goes too, to help look after them. Some of the men are already busy in the fields. They are weeding and watering the wheat.

There is always the danger of wild animals attacking the herd. Tupi scares off a wolf by hurling rocks at it with his sling.

Uncle Ugar paints zig-zag designs on the pots with a brush.

Aunt Esha is grinding the earth into powder. She adds water and fat to make the paint.

Cousin Narvon is coiling a piece of clay into a pot. Then he smooths it down with his fingers.

Most of the men in the village are farmers. But there are a few full-time craftsmen, such as the potter and the carpenter. Tupi's Uncle Ugar is the village potter. He shapes the pots by hand, then paints them and bakes them in an oven. The paint is made from a coloured earth call ochre. It can be red, yellow or white.

Shara stays at home helping her mother and some of the other women. They prepare food, weave baskets and make clothes. The clothes are made of wool or linen. Linen comes from a plant called flax. The flax and wool are spun into thread, then woven into cloth. Most clothes are a natural, off-white colour. But some are dyed with coloured earths or plants.

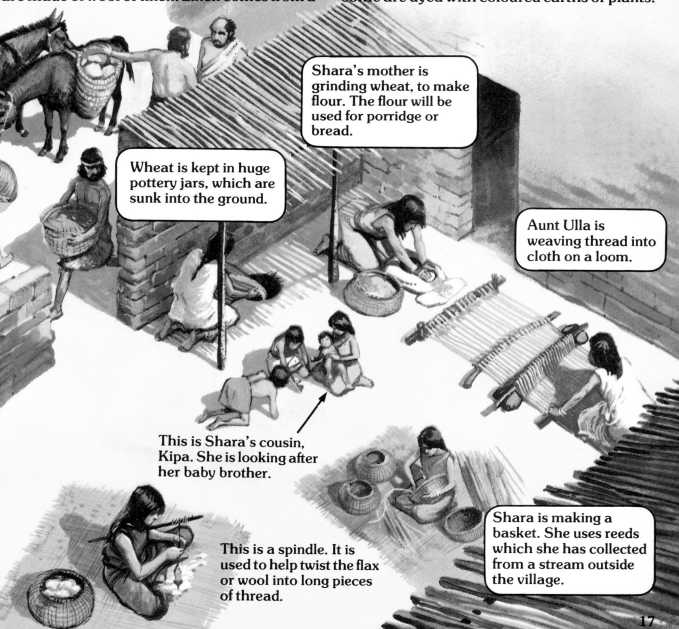

Shara's mother is grinding wheat, to make flour. The flour will be used for porridge or bread.

Wheat is kept in huge pottery jars, which are sunk into the ground.

Aunt Ulla is weaving thread into cloth on a loom.

This is Shara's cousin, Kipa. She is looking after her baby brother.

This is a spindle. It is used to help twist the flax or wool into long pieces of thread.

Shara is making a basket. She uses reeds which she has collected from a stream outside the village.

17

Evening

Before it gets dark, Tupi brings the herd back from the hills. Then he and his brother milk the goats and cows. A lot of the milk will be made into cheese. Milk goes off quickly in the warm weather.

When he has finished his work, Tupi goes to join his friends. They are playing games on the roof. One game is a bit like marbles, played with little stones.

The oven is in the courtyard, because of the danger of the house catching fire.

Shara stirs the stew with a wooden spoon.

Pottery water jar

Food and water are kept in these jars.

The cooking pots are made of pottery. Metal is rare, as there is no metalsmith in the village.

Shara goes down to the well to collect water for cooking and drinking. The washing-up is done in a stream just outside the village walls.

Then she helps her mother cook the supper. It is the main meal of the day. They are having a sort of stew, with beans and barley in it. Shara's mother has made some bread, which she is putting in the oven to bake. The oven is made of clay with a wood fire inside. A small hole in the top lets the smoke out.

There is very little furniture in the house, so the children sit on mats on the floor. They eat the stew from bowls using bread and their fingers. There is barley beer to drink. The second course is fruit, nuts and cheese.

It is starting to get dark, so Tupi's father lights the lamp. It burns oil and fat.

This is a statue of the village goddess. Each day they offer her food and drink. They believe this will please her and bring them luck with the harvest.

They do not stay up late, because it is too dark to see very well. They think it is a waste to keep the lamps lit. The family all sleep in the same room. The beds are straw mats with woollen blankets.

Apricots

Grapes

Dates

Cheese

The bread is flat. They do not know about yeast, which is what makes our bread rise.

19

Shopping

The villagers do not use money. If Tupi's father wants a goat, he might buy one from the man next door and pay for it with bags of wheat. The villagers can produce most of the things they need. Sometimes traders stop at the village. They travel all over the place, exchanging things. There are no fixed prices, so people bargain for things.

The chief is buying slabs of salt. It comes from dried-up salty lakes, many miles away.

Mirror made of obsidian – a black, glassy rock.

Shara wants a turquoise bead to wear round her neck. It is expensive, as it comes all the way from Sinai*.

Obsidian knives

Basket of shells

*Sinai is in modern Egypt.

Beating the copper into flat pieces.

Copper being heated on a fire.

Very few people know how to get metal from rocks and make things with it. There is a metalsmith in the next village. Tupi goes there with his father to buy copper knives and axe-heads. Metal is stronger than the flint, which they normally use.

20

Going hunting

Today Tupi is going hunting with his father and some of the other men. They take their dogs with them. One of Tupi's cousins is looking after his animals for him. Hunting is still a useful way of getting food. The villagers need their animals for milk, wool and for breeding. They cannot afford to kill too many of them.

They go to a lake a few miles from the village. It is a good spot, as a lot of animals come here to drink. Tupi and his father lie in wait under the trees, keeping very quiet. Soon they see a family of gazelles.

Flint arrow-heads

Tupi's father takes aim with his bow and arrow.

Tupi catches a young wolf cub, which has strayed from the pack. He will take it home and train it like one of the dogs.

Uncle Ugar is trapping birds with a net. The net has stone weights on it, so the birds cannot fly away.

On the way home, Tupi collects some wild dates to take back to his mother.

21

Harvest time

When the wheat ripens, it is a busy time for everyone. Women and children put aside their other jobs to join the men in the fields. A lot of fruits and nuts are ready for picking too. Figs, dates, almonds, apricots and walnuts all grow wild here.

Tupi is threshing the wheat with a stick. This is to separate the grain from the stalks.

Shara is tossing the grain in the air. This is called winnowing. It makes the light outer skin blow away.

Fig trees

Date palms

These children are bringing refreshments of bread, cheese and fruit to the harvesters.

The wheat is collected in baskets and loaded onto donkeys.

This woman is gleaning – picking up odd stalks of wheat other people have missed.

Wooden sickles with flint blades are used to cut the wheat.

The grain is then stored in granaries, like these.

Not everyone is lucky enough to have a good harvest. A village across the valley has had no rain all year. Very little has grown, so many of them may starve. They attack Tupi's village in the night, to try to steal the grain supplies. They set fire to some of the houses first, to distract attention. But the villagers chase them away with sticks and stones.

Most of the village escapes damage, but Uncle Ugar's house is nearly destroyed. The family set to work rebuilding it the next day. The walls are made of mud brick, with a coating of mud on top.

Tupi's cousins are mixing mud and straw with their feet. This is then shaped into bricks and left to dry in the sun.

Poles are laid across the tops of the walls, to support the roof.

The roof is coated with mud, then thatched with straw.

23

Harvest festival

When all the wheat has been harvested, there is a ceremony in the village shrine. The villagers thank their goddess for the harvest.

They bring wheat, fruit, beer, animals and flowers for her. The chief and his wife act as priest and priestess, presenting the gifts.

Chief

Tupi has brought one of his sheep.

The walls are painted with red ochre.

Shara is wearing her best dress. It has a zigzag pattern woven into the material.

Tambourine

Flute

Drum

The older men of the village are there to advise the chief.

People also discuss their problems here and settle arguments.

In the evening there is a big party, with lots to eat and drink. Everyone sings and dances round a fire in the centre of the village. Some of the villagers have formed a band, playing flutes, drums, and tambourines.

The next day, the chief holds a meeting of the whole village. It is to decide how the farming land will be divided for the following year. This is done every year, so that everyone has a turn at farming the best land.

24

Living in ROMAN TIMES

Contents

26 Julius and his city
28 The street where Julius lives
30 Getting up
32 Going to school
34 After school
36 The public baths
37 The evening
38 Going shopping
40 Julia's wedding
42 A public holiday
44 Moving house
46 Going on holiday
48 Staying in the country

Julius and his city

This part of the book is all about a nine year old boy called Julius Valerius Cato. He lives in the city of Rome in Italy. The story takes place nearly 2,000 years ago. This was long before things like electricity, cars, aeroplanes or television were invented. The people who lived in Rome were called Romans. They spoke Latin. The Romans had a huge army and ruled most of Europe.

This is Julius and his pet dog, Brutus. Like most Romans, Julius lives in a flat. Only very rich people can afford houses of their own.

Julius's parents are called Antonius and Livia. Antonius works as a banker, lending people money.

Julius has a 15 year old brother, Caius*, and two sisters, Octavia, aged seven and Julia, aged 13.

Several slaves live in the flat too. They do the cooking and the housework and look after the children. A slave is someone who is owned by another person. There are a lot of slaves in Rome. They do all the hard jobs. Many are people from other countries, who were captured by the Romans during wars.

26 *Caius is pronounced Ky-us.

Capitol Hill. This is one of seven hills in Rome.

The baths

This is the temple where Julius's family go to pray. The Romans believe in many different gods and have lots of temples.

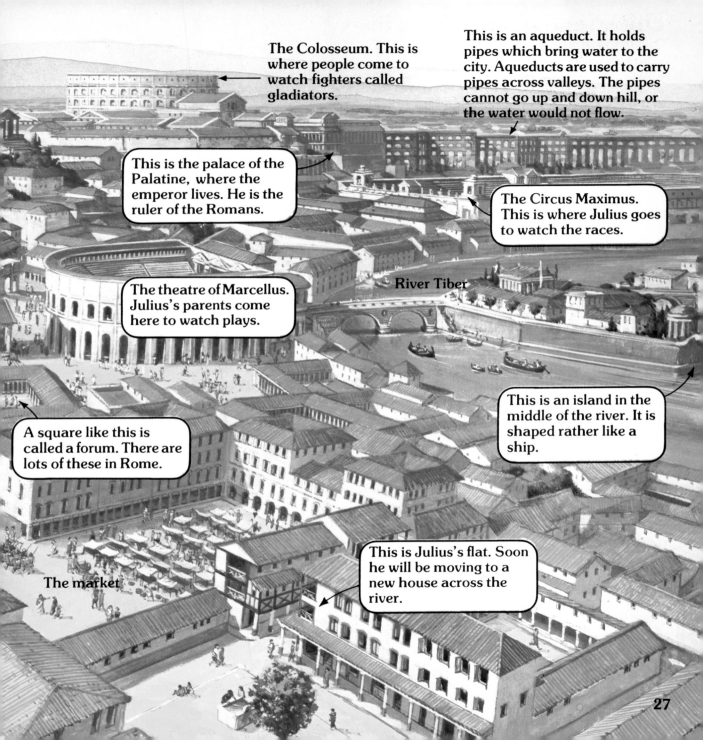

The Colosseum. This is where people come to watch fighters called gladiators.

This is an aqueduct. It holds pipes which bring water to the city. Aqueducts are used to carry pipes across valleys. The pipes cannot go up and down hill, or the water would not flow.

This is the palace of the Palatine, where the emperor lives. He is the ruler of the Romans.

The Circus Maximus. This is where Julius goes to watch the races.

The theatre of Marcellus. Julius's parents come here to watch plays.

River Tiber

This is an island in the middle of the river. It is shaped rather like a ship.

A square like this is called a forum. There are lots of these in Rome.

This is Julius's flat. Soon he will be moving to a new house across the river.

The market

27

The street where Julius lives

This is the block of flats where Julius lives. It is built around a courtyard. Julius's flat is on the first floor. It does not have a name or number. Only the main streets in Rome have names. So it is quite easy to get lost.

A night-watchman patrols the streets at night, making sure the buildings are locked. He has to keep a sharp look out for burglars too.

Opposite the flat is the barber's shop. Julius's father goes there to have his hair cut. It is a good place to meet friends and hear the latest news.

This is Julius's friend, Cornelius. His family rent the flat above from Julius's father.

Julius's bedroom

Baker's shop. Bread is baked here every morning.

Barber's shop

28

This is the dining room. The Romans have their meals lying on couches.

The artist has cut away the walls so you can see the rooms inside the flat.

Most people get their water here. A few flats have their own water supply. The owners pay to have pipes connected to the fountain.

Tavern

The tavern is a noisy, lively place. It sells drinks and cheap, hot meals. Many of the poorer people do not have kitchens in their flats. They eat here instead.

There are no toilets in Julius's flat. But there are some on the ground floor, which are shared by everyone in the block.

Getting up

Julius shares a bedroom with his brother Caius. One of the slaves wakes them when it is time to get up. It is still dark, so he lights an oil lamp.

Everyone gets up early in Rome. The streets start to bustle with people even before it is light. There are no clocks or watches, so no-one knows exactly what the time is. There are no street lights, but people carry lanterns to see by.

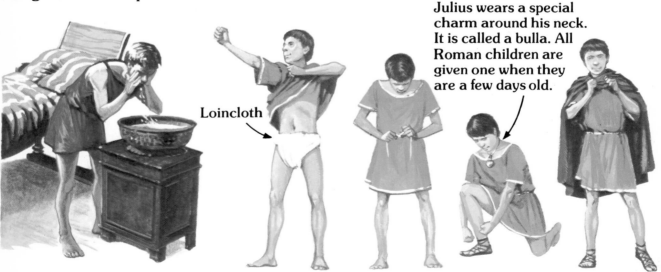

Julius wears a special charm around his neck. It is called a bulla. All Roman children are given one when they are a few days old.

Loincloth

Julius washes his face and hands. He rubs his teeth with his fingers and a special kind of powder.

Then he puts on a clean tunic and laces his leather sandals. When it is cold, he wears a short cloak too. It is very hot in Rome for most of the year, so people do not need to wear many clothes.

Octavia's tunic is made of cool, thin material. Poorer children wear tunics of cheaper material that feels rough and itchy.

She has a woollen belt around her waist.

Shawl

Leather sandals

Octavia puts on a long tunic with a thin tunic underneath. On top of this she wears a shawl. Roman girls dress just like their mothers.

The nurse combs her hair and plaits it for her. Octavia looks at herself in the mirror. It is made of polished silver. Mirror glass has not been invented.

Toga

Julius's father wears a toga over his tunic when he goes out. This is a large piece of cloth which he wraps round his body in a special way. Slaves and people from other countries are not allowed to wear togas.

Every morning the family prays together in the hall. They stand in front of the household shrine. This is the home of the gods who look after the family. The children bring food and drink to offer to the gods.

31

Going to school

Julius is taken to school by his personal slave, Titus. His friend, Cornelius goes with them. They do not have a proper breakfast. Instead they buy some bread to eat on the way. To get to school they walk along the river. There are barges of wheat being unloaded at the docks.

Theatre of Marcellus

Warehouses

These animals have been brought by ship from Africa. They will be used in fights to entertain the public.

Sacks of wheat from Egypt

Roman girls do not go to school. Julia and Octavia are taught at home by their mother. They learn to read, write and run a house. A music teacher comes to give Julia lessons.

Julius's classroom is above a shop. The school is run by a Greek teacher, called Perseus. There is only one class.

Statue of a famous writer.

Caius goes to a secondary school. Here he is learning how to speak in public. Romans think this is very important. He also learns Latin grammar, history, maths and Greek.

Roman numbers look different from ours. These are the numbers from one to ten.

I II III IV V VI VII VIII IX X

The children write on boards covered with wax. They use a pointed stick called a stylus. The flat end is used for rubbing out.

Books are written on scrolls – long rolls of papyrus (a kind of paper).

An abacus for doing sums. You slide the wooden balls along the wire as you count.

There are five boys in Julius's class. Most of them started going to school when they were six. They learn reading, writing and sums. Julius's father has to pay the teacher.

Many Roman children do not go to school as their parents cannot afford it. The teacher is strict. He beats the boys if they do not remember their lessons.

After school

School finishes at about midday. Then Julius and his friends are free to play games in the streets. There is no danger of being run over. Horse-drawn carts and chariots are the only things the Romans have to travel in. These are not allowed in Rome during the day.

The library. Julius's father sometimes comes here to read about the history of Rome.

The baths

Very rich people travel around in carrying chairs, called litters.

Julius and a friend are playing at being gladiators – special fighters who entertain the public.

The boys buy a snack lunch from a shop selling hot food. They have bread, cheese and sausages.

34

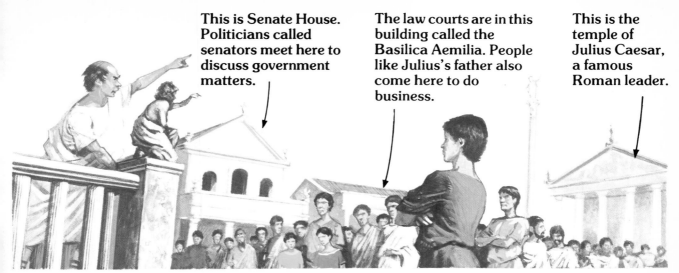

This is Senate House. Politicians called senators meet here to discuss government matters.

The law courts are in this building called the Basilica Aemilia. People like Julius's father also come here to do business.

This is the temple of Julius Caesar, a famous Roman leader.

The boys are not in a hurry to get home. They persuade Titus to take them into the city to explore. They go to the Roman Forum, the main forum in the centre of Rome. There are a lot of temples and other important buildings here. A politician is making a speech. He is a popular man and a lot of people have gathered to hear him.

On the way back, the boys visit Uncle Claudius, who is an army officer. He takes them to the barracks to watch the soldiers training. Like many Roman boys, Julius wants to go into the army one day.

Julius gets home at about four o'clock. He finds his sisters and their friends in the courtyard. They are playing knucklebones, a game rather like dice. You play with four pieces of bone with numbers on each side.

The public baths

There is a pool with very hot water in here.

Cold outdoor pool

Warm indoor pool

Like many Roman men, Julius's father spends most afternoons at the baths. (Women can go in the mornings.) Hardly anyone has a bath at home. People go there to meet friends, not just to wash or swim. There are several different pools, indoors and out. The water varies from very cold to steaming hot. The baths have shops, a library and a sports ground attached to them. Caius goes running and jumping in the sports ground. It is important for him to keep fit. He will be joining the army when he is sixteen.

Before having a swim, Antonius does some wrestling.

Then he goes into the hottest room, the steam room. The steam makes you sweat all the dirt out.

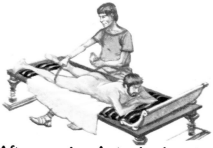

After a swim, Antonius is scrubbed clean by his slave. The slave rubs oil on his skin. Then he scrapes it off with a special scraper.

36

The evening

There is no chimney, so the kitchen gets quite smoky.

The cooking pots are made of clay. They break easily but are cheap to buy.

Before Julius goes to sleep, he asks Titus to tell him a story — one of his favourites about the Trojan Wars. Titus tells it from memory. Books are expensive, as they have to be written by hand.

Julius and Octavia have their supper in the kitchen at about six o'clock. The cooks are busy preparing dinner for the grown-ups and the older children. Many Romans go to bed as soon as it gets dark. They cannot afford to keep their oil lamps burning all evening.

Now it is getting dark and the streets are becoming noisy. Julius can hear the horses and carts bringing goods to market. Suddenly he hears shouting and rushes to the window. A block of flats has caught fire. Firemen are rushing down the street with buckets of water and hoses. There are a lot of fires in Rome. Many flats are built of cheap materials, which catch fire easily. Oil lamps and open stoves can be dangerous.

Going shopping

In Julius's family, the slaves do most of the shopping. But today Julius is going shopping with his mother. He wants to buy a wedding present for his sister, Julia. She is getting married next month.

Julius's mother is buying some material for Julia's wedding dress. It is white silk. This is expensive as it comes all the way from China.

At the glass shop, Julius can see the craftsmen working at the back of the shop. He chooses a coloured glass bowl for his sister.

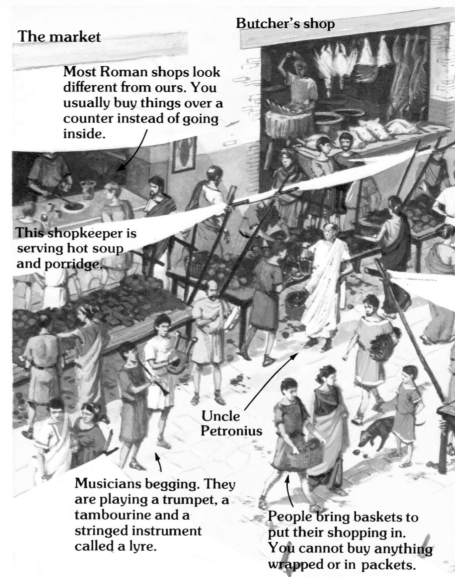

The market

Butcher's shop

Most Roman shops look different from ours. You usually buy things over a counter instead of going inside.

This shopkeeper is serving hot soup and porridge.

Uncle Petronius

Musicians begging. They are playing a trumpet, a tambourine and a stringed instrument called a lyre.

People bring baskets to put their shopping in. You cannot buy anything wrapped or in packets.

In Rome there are lots of different markets. Many of them are open every day. Some sell just fruit and vegetables. Others sell meat or fish. Julius sometimes goes to markets with his Uncle Petronius, who is a market inspector. His job is to check that the food is fresh and correctly weighed.

Stepping stones help you cross the street in wet weather.

This man has been arrested by a soldier for stealing fruit.

Advertisement

These men have no jobs. They queue up every day for free wheat. This is given by the government.

These men are painting an advertisement for the races, which will be held next week.

People pay for things with coins made of bronze, silver or gold. There is no paper money.

This stall is selling fruit called pomegranates. The Romans do not have potatoes or tomatoes. These come originally from South America and have not been discovered yet.

Next they go to the chemist's. Julius has hurt his knee. The chemist mixes an ointment of fat and herbs to put on it.

The togas are whitened over fires burning a chemical called sulphur.

The cloth is trodden in a special mixture to clean it.

A slave takes one of Antonius's togas to the cleaner's. Roman cleaners are called fullers. They use a kind of clay called fuller's earth to clean things.

Julia's wedding

Julia's nails are being painted.

Perfume

Make-up

Today is Julia's wedding day. Octavia and some of the slave women are helping her to get ready. She will wear a white dress and an orange veil with a crown of leaves. Julia is marrying a young nobleman called Lucius Philippus. Like all Roman marriages, it was arranged by the parents.

There is a short ceremony in front of the family shrine. Then the marriage contract is read and signed.

The door is decorated with garlands of leaves.

Lucius and his parents are waiting to greet Julia at the door.

The guests all join in a procession to the bride's new home. Two children take Julia by the hand. Two other children walk behind carrying her things. There are singers and musicians too. Julius leads the procession.

He holds a torch made of burning wood. This is meant to chase away evil spirits. Julia is going to live with Lucius's family. After a special ceremony at the doorway, she is carried into the house.

40

A big party is held in Lucius's house. The children are invited too, as it is a special occasion. Singers, dancers and other entertainers have been hired. Julius likes the acrobats best. The guests lie on couches and eat with their fingers. Slaves bring in huge dishes of food. There are lots of different courses. The slaves wipe the guests' fingers between courses. At the end of the party, everyone is given a special cake to take home with them. It is made of pastry, cooked in wine and wrapped in leaves.

Musicians

Acrobats

There are all kinds of different meat dishes, including wild boar, goat, venison (deer), ostriches and even stuffed mice.

Lobster

This slave is mixing wine and water in a jar called a krater. Everyone drinks this – even the children.

Stuffed pig's head

Uncle Claudius has just come back from fighting in Mesopotamia*. He has bought presents for everyone, including a board game for Julius.

*This is in the Middle East.

A public holiday

Today is a holiday, so Julius is not going to school. The Romans do not have weekends, but they have a lot of public holidays instead. This one is Saturnalia, the festival of the god Saturn. It takes place at about the same time as our Christmas and lasts for several days. Julius has been looking forward to it for a long time.

People decorate their houses, inside and out, with garlands of leaves.

The family give each other presents. Julius gets a hoop from his mother. Octavia is given a wooden doll. The slaves are given the day off and some pocket money to spend.

Their friends and neighbours join in a big procession. It goes to the temple of Saturn. A bull is killed on an altar. This is done as a present for the god.

In the evening there is a big party. Everyone joins in – even the slaves. Julius and his family serve them at supper. Roast baby pig is always eaten on this holiday.

The emperor's palace

For each race, the chariots go round the track seven times. There are about ten races in a day.

The stadium holds 250,000 people. This is a quarter of the number of people who live in Rome.

This is the imperial box. The emperor and his family sit here.

The races can be very dangerous. Bumping and ramming are allowed and there are often accidents. Sometimes the horses or charioteers are killed.

Julius wants the red team to win, so he waves a red scarf.

The chariot drivers wear metal helmets to protect their heads. They have leather bandages wrapped round their chest and legs.

The next day, Julius's father takes the family to the races. They are held in a huge stadium called the Circus Maximus. Four teams of chariots take part. Each team wears a different colour – red, white, blue or green. There is a prize of money for the winner. It costs nothing to get in. Everyone tries to arrive early, in order to get the best seats.

Moving house

Today Julius and his family are moving house. Everyone is very busy, arranging furniture and unpacking. Julius's father has made a lot of money from his work. Now they can afford to move out of their flat into a roomy villa. Last night the slaves loaded everything into carts and brought it over to the new house.

Most of the windows and balconies face on to the inside of the house. This makes it cooler because there is more shade.

The front door is thick and has a big lock, to keep out thieves. One of the slaves acts as doorkeeper.

Roman houses have much less furniture than ours, and no carpets.

Shrine

Julius's father is telling the slaves where to put everything.

This is the atrium, the main hall and sitting room. It has an opening in the roof with a pool underneath to catch the rainwater.

The house has a central heating system. The floors all stand on pillars. A fire burning in the cellar makes hot air. This flows between the pillars and heats the floor above. (The floor has been cut away, so you can see underneath.)

The house is still being decorated. An artist is painting a picture on one of the walls. He wets the plaster first and then paints on to it. He has an assistant to mix the paints.

The floor of the dining room is being covered with mosaics. These are designs made from tiny pieces of coloured stone. Julius is helping the artist to find the right colours.

One of the things Julius likes best about the new house is the garden. There are trees and grapevines and a pool with a fountain. Julius's father has bought two new slaves to work as gardeners. They belonged to the last owner of the house.

Going on holiday

It is August now and very hot in Rome. Julius is going to stay with his grandparents in the country. His father is staying behind. He wants to supervise the decorators in the new house.

Octavia and her mother are travelling in a litter. It is carried by eight slaves.

Julius and his brother are riding on horseback. The luggage comes behind them in a cart.

The woods are full of animals, such as wild boar. These hunters are armed with spears. Guns have not been invented yet.

This coach is taking passengers to the city.

Slaves pull barges full of wheat up the river to Rome.

A few rich people have their own carriages.

You can see tombstones along the road. No-one is buried inside the city.

This chariot is carrying the emperor's mail. There is no postal service for ordinary people.

Most Roman roads are straight. They only bend to go round a big hill.

These workmen are building a new road. They have a special instrument to show when the ground is level.

A farmer is taking vegetables to market in his cart.

The Roman mile is 1,000 paces long. (This is shorter than ours.) Each mile is marked by a milestone, like this one.

Most people travel on foot. They cannot afford any kind of transport.

In the afternoon they stop at Ostia, a seaside port. Julius watches the sailors load the ships with cargo. Some of the ships travel to far-away places, such as India.

Julius's grandparents live on a farm. It is about two days' journey away. The family spend the night at an inn on the way.

Staying in the country

The farm is about five miles from the nearest village. To get there, they have to travel down a long, dusty road. It is a busy time on the farm. The wheat is nearly ready for harvesting. As they arrive, they see slaves picking grapes and olives. Most of the grapes will be made into wine. The olives will be used to make oil. About 100 slaves work on the farm. There are cattle, sheep, geese and chickens too. Julius's father will join them in a few weeks. They will stay until the end of September.

Beehives for making honey.

The slaves sleep here.

These men are collecting olives in baskets.

Stables

Oil and wine are stored in jars dug into the ground.

Julius's cousins have come to stay too. One of them is learning to swim. He uses a float made of reeds to hold on to.

Grandfather spends a lot of time fishing.

The cart will take the olives back to the farm to be crushed.

Picking grapes

LIVING IN CASTLE TIMES

Contents

50 Thomas and his town
52 Thomas's house and family
54 Getting up and going to school
56 At school
57 Alice's lessons
58 Going shopping
60 Dinner time
62 In the workshop
64 Trip to a monastery
66 A village fair
68 Inside the castle
70 Alice's engagement
72 Index

Thomas and his town

This is Thomas Middleton. He is nine years old. In this book you can find out all about Thomas and his family. They lived about 600 years ago. The big picture shows you the town where they lived.

In Thomas's time life was very different from nowadays. Here are some of the things that were different:

✱ There were no cars, lorries, buses, trains or bicycles. People used horses, carriages and carts instead.

✱ There were no televisions, radios, telephones or newspapers and hardly any books. Messengers carried letters and town criers shouted out the latest news.

✱ People had no electricity or gas for lights, cooking and heating. They used open fires, candles and lamps.

✱ There was no running water in the houses. People had to fetch it from wells and rivers. Most people did not have baths or wash very often and most things were much dirtier and smellier than they are now.

Lord John lives at the castle. He owns most of the land outside the town walls.

People practise archery in this open space.

There are four gates in the wall. This is one of them. Strangers have to pay to come through them. They are guarded all the time and locked up at night.

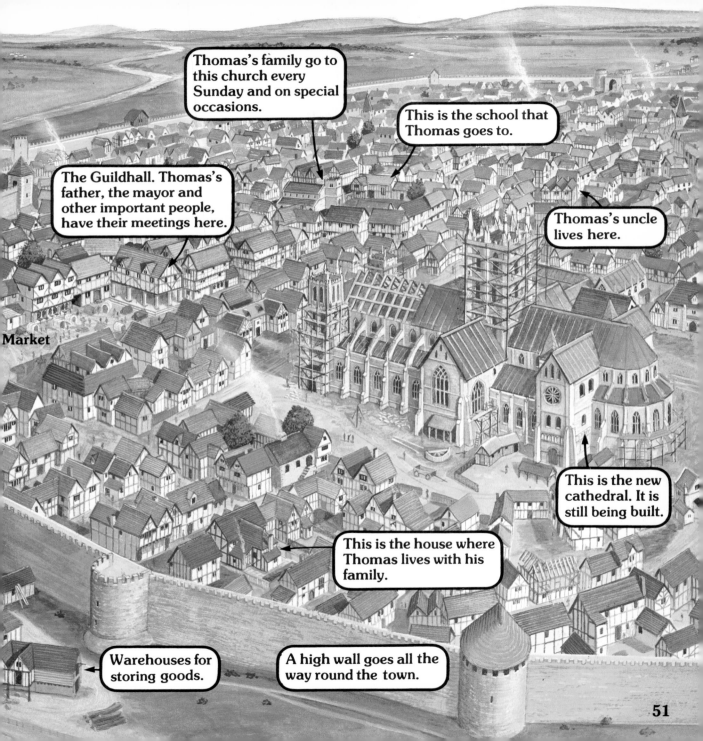

51

Thomas's house and family

Here are the people in Thomas's family.

Thomas's father, Master Middleton, is a goldsmith. His mother, Mistress Middleton, is always busy with the jobs that need doing around the house.

Thomas has one brother and one sister. His brother, Hugh is 14 and his sister, Alice is 12.

This is the house where Thomas lives with his family. We have taken one side wall away so that you can see all the rooms.

Thomas and his brother, Hugh, sleep in the attic.

This room is called the solar. It is Master and Mistress Middleton's bedroom and it is also used as a family living room. Alice has a bed in one corner.

The front part of the workshop is a shop. It has a wooden counter that opens out on to the street.

In the workshop the journeymen and apprentices make things from gold.

The servants, journeymen and apprentices sleep on the floor in the hall and the workshop.

Herbs, vegetables and flowers grow in the garden.

Kitchen

This is the hall, where the family eat their meals and entertain visitors.

Here are some of the other people who live and work in the Middleton's house.

The maid, Nan, and her husband, Dick, do most of the cooking and cleaning.

The two journeymen*, Will and Walter, work for Master Middleton in his goldsmith's workshop.

Ned and Nick are both 14. They are Master Middleton's apprentices. They help in the workshop and are learning to be goldsmiths. They do not get paid.

*Journeymen are trained craftsmen who work for other people in return for wages.

53

Getting up and going to school

Everyone gets up very early in the morning. In the winter it is still dark when Thomas wakes up.

Nan pours the water into a bowl and the boys scramble out of bed and splash their faces with it. Soap is expensive so they only use it on special occasions.

At five o'clock, Nan, the maid, comes into the room Thomas shares with his brother, Hugh. She brings a jug filled with cold water from a well in the garden.

She opens the wooden shutters that cover the window at night. Sometimes she has to shake the boys and splash them with water to wake them up.

As he hurries along, he usually passes Gilbert Star, the nightwatchman. Gilbert has patrolled the streets all night, making sure everything is peaceful.

On the way to school Thomas goes past the place where the new cathedral is being built. The workmen are already hard at work. Thomas loves to stand and watch them. He does not stay too long because he is frightened of being late for school.

Thomas fetches his clothes from a peg on the wall. He takes off his nightshirt and pulls on his thick woollen tunic and hose (tights) and his leather shoes.

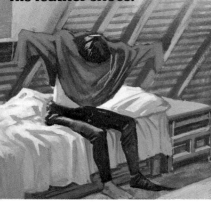

There are no bathrooms or toilets inside the Middleton's house, but there is a toilet in a wooden shed, which has been built on to the side of the house.

Thomas does not have much breakfast before he goes to school. He goes into the kitchen and grabs a hunk of bread and some cheese to eat on his way.

The street is already very busy. Thomas has to keep dodging out of the way of carts and packhorses. People from the countryside are bringing animals, vegetables and other food to sell in the markets and shops.

People throw all their rubbish out of their windows into the streets. They usually give a warning shout so you can jump out of the way, but it makes the streets very smelly.

At school

Thomas arrives at school just before the clock strikes six. It is next to St Peter's Church and is called St Peter's Grammar School. There are about 90 boys divided into three classes.

The master at the school is the priest at St Peter's Church. He has two assistants to help him teach. They are both training to be priests.

Books are very expensive because they have to be written by hand. Only the master has a book. It is made out of parchment (animal skin).

The boys write on slates covered with wax. The wax can be melted and smoothed, so the slate can be used lots of times.

All the lessons are in Latin and the boys are supposed to speak only Latin all the time they are at school. The master reads out passages from a book and the boys learn them by heart.

The master is very strict. If a boy does not learn his lesson well, he beats him with a bunch of sticks. He also beats them if they are late or forget to speak in Latin.

56

Alice's lessons

While Thomas is out at school, his sister, Alice, stays at home. First she helps her mother with all the things that need doing in the house, so that when she gets married she will know how to run her own house. Then she has some lessons.

In the kitchen they check the stores of food and drink and decide what extra supplies they need to buy.

They collect herbs and ▶ flowers from the garden. Some of these they scatter on the floor in the house to make it smell nice.

◀ They check that Nan has swept out all the rooms. The hall floor is covered with rushes to mop up food and dirt and these have to be changed once a week.

Alice's mother shows her how to crush herbs and use them with other ingredients to make medicines for the family. ▼

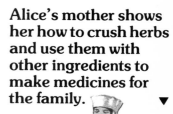

Alice has already learnt how to sew. She helps with the clothes that need mending. She also decorates linen and wallhangings with elaborate embroidery.

Her mother is teaching her how to read and write. She does not enjoy it much, but her mother makes her practise every day. ▼

▲ When she has finished her writing lesson, her music tutor arrives. He teaches her how to play tunes on the instrument shown in this picture, which is called a psaltery. He also gives her singing lessons.

Going shopping

When she has finished her lessons, Alice often goes shopping with her mother.

All shops selling the same type of things are gathered together in one street.

Each shop has a painted picture sign to show what it sells, because most people cannot read.

The shops are very small. The shopkeepers keep their goods in the front part of their houses.

Alice and her mother are buying some cloth. They will take it to a tailor and ask him to make Alice a new dress.

Wooden shutters from the windows let down to make counters, which stick out into the street.

This is a barber's shop. The barber is about to give this man a shave.

This woman is selling fresh fruit from the countryside.

Hot pie seller

Beggar

People often carry bunches of herbs or flowers to smell, because the streets smell so filthy.

You have to watch out for thieves and pickpockets.

Pillory

Nan, the maid, goes to the market to buy fresh meat and vegetables for dinner.

This butcher has been caught selling rotten meat. As a punishment he has been put in the pillory, where people throw rotten meat at him.

While his mother and sister are shopping, Thomas is on his way back from school. He takes the long way home, so he can watch people practising archery in the field below the castle.

When he arrives home he finds Ned and Nick playing ball in the street with some other apprentices. He joins in. The games are very rough and often end in fights. He hopes his father does not catch them playing.

59

Dinner Time

Dinner is at six o'clock in the Middleton's house. It is the main meal of the day. In the kitchen Nan and Dick are busy getting it ready. Mistress Middleton is making sure they do everything right.

In this pot, a stew is cooking.

Dick is taking some fruit pies out of the oven.

Dirty dishes

A joint of beef and some birds are roasting over the open fire. They are fixed on to a metal rod called a spit.

Nan is chopping herbs from the garden to make sauces for the meat.

The family drink wine out of pewter goblets. The children mix water with their wine.

Each person has a knife, a spoon and a plate. These are made of pewter (a mixture of tin and lead). There are no forks.

People throw their scraps and bones on the floor and the dogs eat them up.

Everyone who lives in the house eats together. Members of the family and guests sit at the top table. Servants, journeymen

Thomas is holding a basin of water for a guest at the top table. Everyone washes their hands and dries them on napkins.

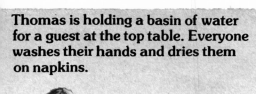

Hugh carves the meat before passing it round.

The servants eat off wooden plates and drink beer from clay mugs.

Each person has a thick slice of bread to eat with their meat. There are no potatoes in Europe at this time.

and apprentices sit at the lower table. Before anyone sits down Master Middleton says a prayer.

After dinner Thomas and Alice play with their toys before going to bed.

Thomas has some toy soldiers made out of wood and string. When you pull the strings their arms and legs move.

Alice has a pet bird in a cage. Her father bought it for her the last time there was a fair in the town.

Hugh has a chess set. He is teaching Thomas how to play.

These are Alice's dolls. They have wooden heads and their bodies are made of cloth stuffed with straw.

Sometimes in the summer they play outside in the garden with wooden bats and balls.

In the workshop

Thomas's brother, Hugh, does not go to school anymore. He works in his father's workshop. One day he will take over the business from his father and run it all by himself.

In the workshop they make jewellery and jugs and plates for noblemen and churches. They work very hard every day except for Sundays.

Master Middleton is talking to the bishop of Castletown about some cups and plates he has ordered.

All the men in the town who work in a trade are members of a kind of club, called a guild. There is a different guild for every trade. This year Master Middleton was chosen as the leader of the Goldsmith's Guild. They meet in the Goldsmith's Hall and make rules that all the members have to obey.

In each guild there are master craftsmen, journeymen and apprentices. The apprentices of one guild often get into fights with apprentices from another guild or with students from the university.

Walter is decorating a gold cup with jewels.

Will is heating up gold in a small pot over the stove.

Hugh is pouring the liquid gold into moulds to make plates.

Nick is carving a pattern round the edge of a gold plate.

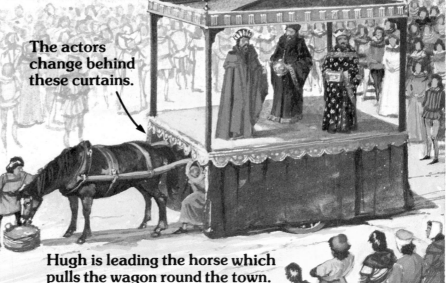

Every Easter there is a special festival. All the guilds put on plays. Each guild acts a different story from the Bible. The goldsmiths are doing the story of the three wise men. They do the plays in the street on wooden carts called pageants. People from all the nearby villages come to town to see the plays. Women are not allowed to belong to the guild, so boys take any women's parts.

The actors change behind these curtains.

Hugh is leading the horse which pulls the wagon round the town.

63

Trip to a monastery

When Thomas is older he is going to work for his Uncle Roger, who is a wool merchant. Today he is setting off on a trip to the countryside to buy wool. Thomas is allowed to go with him.

They are taking several packhorses with them to carry the wool back to the town.

Warehouse by the river where wool is stored.

Abbey church

Refectory (monks' dining room)

Guest house for visitors and travellers.

Dormitory (monks' bedroom)

Monks working in the fields.

After a long day of riding along rough tracks they arrive at Farland Abbey. This is a monastery, where monks live and work together. Uncle Roger is going to buy wool from the monks.

The Abbot (the head of the monastery) meets them at the main gates. He takes them to the guest house, where they are going to stay the night. People travelling on long journeys often stay in the monks' guest house.

The next morning Uncle Roger buys the wool he wants and the servants load up the packhorses. Meanwhile, one of the monks takes Thomas to have a look round the monastery.

First they look inside the church. The monks spend a lot of time every day praying and singing here.

In the library there are some beautiful books made by the monks. Printing has not yet been invented. To make a new copy of a book the monks have to write out each word by hand.

The monks look after sick people in a special part of the monastery called the infirmary. They treat them with medicines made from herbs. There are hardly any hospitals at this time.

The monks also help poor people who have nowhere else to go. At the abbey gates they hand out left-over food and a small sum of money, known as a dole, to anyone they think deserves it.

Trip to a village

Thomas and Uncle Roger are arriving at the village of Longford. They are going to buy some more wool here before travelling home.

Tomorrow is the day of the Longford fair. People are travelling from far and wide to buy and sell things at the fair.

This is a friar. He travels round the country preaching sermons.

Juggler

Wrestling match

The fair starts as soon as it is light the next day. Many of the villagers are selling things they have grown or made. Merchants have brought all sorts of rare goods from distant places.

There are also jugglers, fortune-tellers and other entertainers. Uncle Roger is buying wool from the Lord of the Manor's bailiff (the man who manages all the lord's land and property).

They arrive at the village inn just as a party of pilgrims ride up. They are on their way to a holy place to show their devotion to God. The inn is very crowded so some of them will have to sleep on the floor.

They all have supper in the inn together and Thomas enjoys hearing the stories about things that have happened to the pilgrims on their journey. They have already been travelling for several weeks.

Dancing bear

Acrobats

Tinker selling pots and pans.

Pickpocket

Thomas is buying some ribbons to take back as a present for his sister, Alice.

Merchant selling cloth and brightly-coloured ribbons.

Inside the castle

The guards are expecting them and pull up the portcullis to let them through the gate. In the courtyard servants hurry forward to hold their horses' heads, while they dismount. Lord John and Henry come forward to greet them.

Portcullis

The castle walls are very thick.

Today Master Middleton is going to visit Lord John in his castle. Hugh and Thomas are going with their father. Master Middleton is going to arrange for his daughter, Alice, to be married to Lord John's son, Henry.

Lord John takes Master Middleton to the great hall to discuss the marriage. Master Middleton promises to provide a large dowry (sum of money) with Alice, when the marriage takes place. They agree that Alice and Henry are too young to be married for a few years yet, but decide to celebrate their engagement with a tournament and banquet.

While their fathers are busy, Henry takes Hugh and Thomas to have a look round the castle. They have never been inside it before. Here he is leading them up a spiral staircase to the battlements.

At the top of the staircase the boys come out on an open walk which runs right round the castle walls. Soldiers, armed with bows and arrows and pikes, keep watch day and night.

They go back down to the very bottom of the staircase and arrive at the castle dungeons. Here outlaws who have robbed and killed people on Lord John's lands are kept chained to the walls.

Next Henry takes them to see the armourer's workshop. The armourer and his assistants make and repair all the bows, arrows, pikes, swords and armour for the soldiers who guard the castle.

Blacksmith

Falconer

Then they go to the stables. Lord John has several horses for himself and his family and each knight who lives in the castle has his own horse. Next door to the stables are the kennels. Here the hunting dogs are kept.

Falcons for hunting are kept in buildings called mews. They are used for catching other birds and small animals. Lord John and his followers spend a lot of time out hunting. Sometimes they catch deer and wild boars.

Alice's engagement

On the day of the engagement, Alice and her mother are carried to the castle in a litter. Master Middleton and the boys ride in front. Everyone is wearing their best clothes and Alice has a new dress on.

In the great hall of the castle Lord John and Master Middleton sign documents containing all the details of the marriage agreement. Then Alice and Henry give each other rings.

The area where the fight takes place is called the lists.

Crests on their helmets help people to tell which knight is which.

A wooden barrier called the tilt stops the horses crashing into each other.

To celebrate the engagement a tournament is held in the field below the castle wall. The guests watch from covered stands while knights on horseback charge at each other with long lances and try to knock each other to the ground.

Henry is not a knight yet. He is still a squire, whose job is to serve a knight. When he is older his father will knight him and he will be called Sir Henry. When he marries Alice, she will become Lady Alice.

After the tournament everyone goes back to the castle for a magnificent banquet. It is held in the great hall and will last for several hours. The Middletons sit with Lord John's family on the high table.

Pages and squires wait on the knights

Musicians play in the minstrels' gallery.

Index

abacus, 33
Alps, 12
apprentices, 52, 53, 59, 61, 62
archery, 50, 59
armour, 69
armourer, 69
army, 26, 35, 36
atrium, 44
aqueduct, 27

baker's shop, 28
banquet, 68, 71
barber's shop, 28
barley, 15, 18
Basilica Aemilia, 35
basket making, 17
basket traps, 11
bathing, 13
baths, 26, 34, 36
bear, 3, 4
Bear Clan, 3, 11, 12
beer, 19
bison, 3
books, 33, 37, 56, 65
bow and arrow, 13, 21
bread, 18, 19
bulla, 33
butcher's shop, 38

Capitol Hill, 26
carriages, 46
carts, 55
castle, 50, 68
cathedral, 51
caves, 3, 4, 6-7, 8, 9
cave painting, 8

central heating, 44
chamois, 3
chariots, 43, 46
chemist's shop, 39
China, 38
church, 51, 64, 65
Circus Maximus, 27, 43
cleaner's shop, 39
clothes, 30, 31, 55
    making, 7, 17
Colosseum, 27
cooking, 6-7, 18, 37
copper, 20
cow, 15
crest, 71

dates, 19, 21, 22
digging stick, 5
dining room, 29
dinner, 60, 61
docks, 32
dogs, 15, 16, 21
dole, 65
dowry, 68
drink, 60, 61
drum, 24
duck, 15
dungeons, 69

Egypt, 32
emperor, 27, 43
engagement, 68, 70

fair, 66, 67
Falcons, 69
farming, 14-15, 16, 22-23, 24

farms, 48
fire, making, 4
firemen, 37
fishing, 11
flax, 17
flint, 6, 10, 21, 22
flowers, 53, 57, 59
flute, 24
food, 29, 37, 38, 39, 41, 42, 55, 60, 61
forum, 27, 35
fountain, 29, 45
France, 2
friar, 66
fullers, 39

gazelles, 21
games, 34, 35
gladiators, 27, 34
gleaning, 22
goat, 15, 16
goddess, 15, 19, 24
gods, 27, 31, 42
goldsmith, 52, 62, 63
goose, 15
granaries, 22
Greek, 32, 33
guild, 62, 63
guildhall, 51

hall, 53
harpoon, 10, 11
Herbs, 53, 57, 59, 60
horse, 3, 13
house, 14-15
    building, 23
hunting, 2, 3, 5, 9, 10, 13, 21, 46, 69

huts, 2, 12

India, 47
infirmary, 65
inn, 67

jewellery, 6, 10, 20
journeymen, 52, 53, 60, 62
Julius Caesar, 35

kitchen, 53, 60
knight, 69, 71
knucklebones, 35
krater, 41

lamps, 30, 37
Latin, 26, 33, 56
law courts, 35
leather, making, 13
lessons, 56, 57
library, 34, 36, 65
linen, 17
lists, 70
litter, 70
litters, 34, 46
loom, 17

mammoth, 3, 6, 10
Marcellus, theatre of, 27, 32
markets, 27, 38-39, 47, 55, 59
marriage, 68
master craftsmen, 62
mayor, 51
meals, 55, 60, 61
medicines, 57, 65

merchants, 66, 67
Mesopotamia, 41
metalsmith, 20
mews, 69
milestones, 47
monastery, 64, 65
money, 39
monks, 64, 65
mosaics, 45
mud bricks, 23
music, 57, 71
musicians, 38, 41

night-watchman, 28, 54
numbers, 33

obsidian, 20
ochre, 16, 24
olives, 48
Ostia, 47
outlaws, 69

packhorses, 55, 64, 65
pageants, 63
papyrus, 33
painting, 45
palace of the Palatine, 27, 43
pickpockets, 59, 67
pigs, 15
pilgrims, 67
pillary, 59
port, 47
portcullis, 68
potatoes, 39
pottery, 14, 16

prayers, 31
priests, 56
procession, 40, 42
psaltery, 57

races, 27, 43
reindeer, 3, 5
Reindeer Clan, 2
River Tiber, 27, 32, 46
roads, 46-47
rubbish, 55
rushes, 57

salmon, 3, 11
salt, 20
Saturn, god, 42
Saturnalia, holiday, 42
school, 51, 56
Senate House, 35
senators, 35
servants, 60
sewing, 7
sheep, 15, 16
shells, 6, 7, 13, 20
shops, 28, 34, 38-39, 55, 58
shrine, 15, 24, 31, 41, 44
shutters, 54, 58
sickle, 22
Sinai, 20
slates, 56
slaves, 26
soap, 54
solar, 52
spears, 5, 10

spear-throwing, 5, 6
spindle, 17
spirits, 8, 9
spit, 60
squire, 71
stylus, 33
swapping, 6, 13, 20

tailor, 58
tambourine, 24
tavern, 29
temples, 26, 35, 42
tent, 4, 6
theatre of Marcellus, 27, 32
thieves, 59
threshing, 22
Tiber, River, 27
toga, 31
toilets, 29, 55
tombstones, 46
tools, making, 6, 10, 20
tournament, 68, 70, 71
toys, 61
traders, 20
transport, 46-47
traps, 9, 10, 21
Turkey, 14
turquoise, 20

villa, 44-45
village, 14-15

warehouses, 51, 64
water supply, 29
weapons, 69

weaving, 17
weir, 11
well, 18, 54
wheat, 15, 22-23
whistle, 6
wild boar, 7
winnowing, 22
witch-doctor, 9
wolf, 3, 16
wool, 17, 64, 65, 66
workshop, 52, 53, 62, 63